How to Write Killer Cover Letters & Resumes

How to Write Killer Cover Letters & Resumes

Get the Interviews for the Dream Jobs
You Really Want by Creating
One-in-a-Hundred Job Application Materials

by Richard J. Scholl

AUTHOR™
& COMPANY

Connecticut • New York • Colorado

RICHARD J. SCHOLL

HOW TO WRITE KILLER
COVER LETTERS & RESUMES
Get the Interviews for the Dream Jobs
You Really Want by Creating
One-in-a-Hundred Job Application Materials

Copyright © 2014 by Richard J. Scholl

Int'l ISBN: 978-1-62071-129-3
ISBN: 1-62071-129-X

For information address:
Author & Company, LLC
P.O. Box 291
Cheshire, CT 06410-9998

This book was designed by iLN™

Contents

Author's Note vi

CHAPTER 1
Introduction: The Challenge 1

CHAPTER 2
The Killer Cover Letter 2

CHAPTER 3
Overall Tips 4

CHAPTER 4
Sample of a Typical Cover Letter 6

CHAPTER 5
Killer Cover Letter Examples 8

CHAPTER 6
Effective Resume Examples 23

CHAPTER 7
Final Words 31

CHAPTER 8
Additional Tips to Get Interviews 32

About Richard J. Scholl 34

Author's Note

Stand out from all the rest by crafting cover letters and resumes that will blow people away.

This how-to manual provides a simple, compelling and foolproof way to create job application materials that are uniquely powerful and, most importantly, virtually guaranteed to get you the high value interviews for the jobs you really want.

If you follow the tips and strategies—and apply the principles shown in the sample cover letters and resumes—you can position yourself to command the attention of hiring managers, recruiters and the individual to whom you will be reporting.

You will be empowered to write about yourself as you never have before.

How can you be sure? Take a look at the testimonials sprinkled throughout this manual.

This manual presents proven methods that really work.

You will get interviews—but only if you follow the steps presented in this manual.

Note: all sample cover letters and resumes are inspired by—and adapted from—student work. So they are similar to the work created by Professor Scholl's students and therefore valid and hopefully valuable templates for you. The principles and samples can be applied to any job seeker at any stage in your career.

```
TESTIMONIAL

Professor Scholl,

Not only did my cover letter strike the interest of the CFO, but
by the end of my interview and taking the tour of the company's
facilities, it had reached the hands of the Chairman, CEO, and VP
of accounting and finance, who then all asked to speak with me one
on one while I was there. The interview was nothing but positive.
Thank you again for your help.

Mike Kemske
```

How to Write Killer
Cover Letters & Resumes

CHAPTER 1

Introduction: The Challenge

What is the single best way to get interviews for the jobs you really want?

An estimated 70% of all positions are filled through networking—that is, you get the interview through someone you know. It could be your uncle's friend who happens to be a VP where you want to work. It could be a connection on LinkedIn. In any case, you get the interview because of your network. So you need to make a list of everyone you know and contact them. Don't be afraid to follow up periodically. And keep working the network until you get a job.

Whether you use networking or simply apply for jobs online, the best way to differentiate yourself is with highly effective and very strategically written job application materials—particularly your cover letter. In my experience and based on feedback from students who get hired for really good jobs, the cover letter is the best way to differentiate yourself, to stand out from all the rest.

Your mission is to maximize the number of interviews you get so you have the best chance of receiving an offer. But how do you do that?

Many companies now use systems to look for keywords in job application materials to try to eliminate those who aren't qualified for a given position. But this obstacle is easy to overcome, as you will soon discover. In any case, a recruiter or hiring manager within a company probably receives hundreds of letters and resumes for the typical entry-level opening.

Now put yourself in this individual's shoes. He or she wants to eliminate candidates as quickly as possible and identify the chosen few who will be interviewed. According to a well-publicized study, the hiring manager spends only six seconds on average in evaluating the resume. This particular study doesn't mention cover letters, which are the best way to command the hiring manager's attention.

But let's think about the challenge. Let's say there are 600 applicants for a position. Generally about half will be qualified, but that still leaves 300 for the hiring manager to wade through. How can you be among the 10 or so lucky individuals who will be interviewed? You need to write a killer cover letter and differentiate yourself.

Is this hard or easy? Both. It's easy because if you just do a few things right, you'll differentiate yourself from the 99% who write boring, predictable and often-vague cover letters that sound pretty much like all the others.

CHAPTER 2

The Killer Cover Letter

A killer cover letter is maybe one in 100. They're rare because hardly anyone knows how to write a good to great letter. And they're much harder to write than the typical lame letter. That's because the killer cover letter has one or more of the following characteristics:

1. It is exceptionally well written. That takes time and effort. But it can be done.

2. It is fully customized for each company and position you're applying for.

3. The letter contains keywords to get through the computer screening.

4. You follow a strategic methodology:

   - Address your letter to an individual, even if a name isn't provided. Frequently, you'll be applying online and will simply hit an "Apply" button. Or you'll have an email address but no name. Call the company and ask for the name of the hiring manager for the particular position. You might still apply online without a name and then address a separate communication to an individual. This will differentiate you, even if the individual isn't doing the hiring. If it's the director of the department in which you are applying, that individual will likely get your materials into the right hands. Those materials will be all by themselves, not in a stack of 300 others.

     Note: another way to achieve this kind of differentiation is to apply online and then hand deliver your letter and resume, preferably addressed to an individual. Many people I know have followed this advice and received interviews and offers. Anything you can do that shows genuine effort and interest in the company/position will differentiate you.

   - Accomplish most of the following strategic steps—which virtually anyone can theoretically accomplish—and you will get interviews:

     ✓ FIRST PARAGRAPH. If you have been referred to the company/position, begin with something like this: "James McCarthy, your vice president of operations, recommended that I apply for your entry level marketing coordinator position." A referral is a powerful differentiator that will usually get you the interview.

       Also in first paragraph:

       - State the position and where you found the job opening.

       - Demonstrate knowledge of the company by doing a little research. Go on the web site. Explore. Look for financial information including the annual report. Look at news releases and articles in the media. Get a feel for the company's mission and priorities.

- Say something nice about them, especially if it's something meaningful to you that makes you want to work there.

- Briefly highlight your qualifications.

✓ BODY PARAGRAPHS. After reading the job description several times and highlighting all the words (keywords) that you can speak to in your letter (and resume), make sure these words appear in your job application materials, particularly in the body paragraphs of your letter. Not only will you be far more likely to get through the computer screening for keywords, but you will also demonstrate to the hiring manager that you are well qualified for the position.

After all, the hiring manager may know nothing about your field, but this individual is very familiar with the job description and will most likely only select those who have demonstrated that they have read the job description carefully and are responding very specifically to it.

The exceptionally well-written body paragraphs (and the opening paragraph) make it easy for the hiring manager (and others who may be involved in deciding who gets interviewed) to choose you. Very few people do this well. You can be among those who do.

✓ CLOSING PARAGRAPH. Your cover letter should fit on one page with minimum 11 pt. font size. And, if you write a letter like the samples in this manual, you may not have much room for a closing paragraph of more than a few lines of text. You should definitely:

- Ask for an interview in a confident way and provide your contact information. You should also say "Thank you" at the end.

You might also:

- Briefly reinforce your interest in the company/position and why you're qualified.

CHAPTER 3

Overall Tips

- Companies want to know that you are specifically and genuinely interested in working for them. This is one reason why the letter must be fully customized. Very few applicants communicate real interest in a given company; most simply crank out dozens of nearly generic letters that have no impact. Hiring managers can spot them from a thousand miles away.

- Invest the time and effort in writing killer job application materials, particularly the cover letter. Spend hours, if necessary, on each one. Make sure that you are really and truly interested in the position. Otherwise, you won't be motivated to produce your best writing.

- The best cover letters create a connection between the applicant and the company/position. The hiring manager and others in the company can picture you in the job, performing well and contributing to the team and the organization's success. Try to create a kind of portrait of yourself that is appealing, compelling and relevant.

- Demonstrate what you can do for the company, not what they can do for you. Talk about the contribution you can make. This is what they care about. They want valuable employees, and they're not easy to find.

- Proofread. Proofread some more. Have someone else proofread. Spell check. If you have even one typo, you will almost certainly not get interviewed.

Professor Scholl,

I would like to thank you for the skills of writing an effective cover letter and resume. I used these to apply for a promotion within my company and was interviewed the same day that I submitted it. By the end of the interview, I was offered this position and accepted.

Sincerely,

Aaron Emmons

Two emails received:

1st:

My first interview for the job was with the CEO of the company, and the first thing he mentioned was how well written my cover letter and resume were (and how that was such a huge factor, given the nature of the position).

2nd:

I got a really good job offer yesterday for a technical writing position at the company I wanted to work for. I went in today to be taken out to lunch by the CEO and accept the offer.

Thanks for all your help! It must have been my rock star cover letter.

Take care,

Mary Bachman

Hello Professor Scholl,

I just wanted to inform you about a success in my career due to your outstanding ENG 368 course this past semester. I have just been hired at SEPTA in Philadelphia as a summer intern in their Budget Department. It is a very incredible opportunity, but here's the best part-they didn't have a summer internship position in any finance related field until they read my cover letter and decided to create one just for me!

My aunt is employed at SEPTA, which was surely also helpful in me getting this position, but she said they were truly blown away by my cover letter. I heard all of your examples in class on the first few days, but I never really understood until now how important a great cover letter is to receiving a job in this rough economy.

Also, in my cover letter, I did exactly what you taught us in class by applying and "creating our own job" if one was not available in our field. I applied for an IT position even though I have no knowledge in that field. However, the letter obviously got into the correct person's hands because they were able to pass it along far enough to create an entirely new position in their company.

Thank you SO SO SO SO much for all of your help! I am beyond excited for this opportunity and so thankful for all of your help.

Have a great summer,

Amy Pisciella
Applied Mathematics Major
West Chester University, Honors Student Association

CHAPTER 4

Sample of a Typical Cover Letter

See why it's easy for the hiring manager to reject this applicant in seconds.

Sue Mason

2750 Tower Ave., #58 | Sometown, CO 50805
Home: 555-555-5555 | Cell: 555-555-5500
Email: someone@somedomain.com

[Date]

Ms. Rhonda Quest
Customer Service Manager
Acme Inc.
123 Corporate Blvd.
Sometown, CO 50802

Re: Customer Service Representative Opening (Ref. ID: CS300-Denver)

Dear Ms. Quest:

I saw your job opening for a customer service representative, and I hope to be invited for an interview.

I have served as a customer service associate within retail environments and call centers. Most recently, I worked on the customer service desk for a discount store, and my responsibilities included processing customer merchandise returns, issuing refunds and credits, flagging defective merchandise for shipment back to vendors and cashiering during busy periods.

Previously, I worked within two high-volume customer-support call centers for a major cable and a satellite television services provider. In these positions, I demonstrated the ability to resolve a variety of issues and complaints (such as billing disputes, service interruptions or cutoffs, repair technician delays/ no-shows and equipment malfunctions). I consistently met my call-volume goals, handling an average of 62 to 66 calls daily.

I also gained considerable customer service while working as a waitress and restaurant hostess while in high school.

I also bring to the table strong computer proficiencies in MS Word, MS Excel and CRM database applications and a year of college (business major). Please see the accompanying resume for details of my experience and education.

I am confident that I can offer you the customer service, communication and problem-solving skills you are seeking. Feel free to call me at 555-555-5555 (home) or 555-555-5500 (cell) to arrange an interview. Thank you for your time—I look forward to learning more about this opportunity!

Sincerely,

Sue Mason
Enclosure: Resume

CALLOUTS:

[first paragraph]

Opening paragraph is me-oriented. There is no evidence that she researched the company or truly wants to work there. She also doesn't indicate how she learned about the job. This opening makes it easy for the hiring manager to reject the applicant quickly, despite her excellent qualifications.

[body paragraphs]

In her body paragraphs—two through four—the applicant provides what appear to be good qualifications and experience. However, there is no matching between her and the job description because she never mentions it or what the company is looking for. As a result, she may not even make it through computer screening because she may not have keywords from the job description in these body paragraphs. And all the hiring manager has is the job description, so he or she is looking for language from that job description.

[final paragraph]

This is not bad. She summarizes the reasons why she should be interviewed and provides her contact information. She also comes across as confident and enthusiastic. But I would avoid exclamation points in job application materials; if you're excited about an opportunity, that will come through in your writing; if you aren't, all the exclamation points in the world won't help.

Overview:

Too me-oriented. Not the type of letter that stands out from the pack. Easily rejected.

CHAPTER 5

Killer Cover Letter Examples

Observations:

See why the best cover letters get interviews. And feel free to mimic aspects of these letters that work for you. That doesn't mean that you copy what others have done. You simply pay attention to what is most effective and creatively do something similar—or better—in your own cover letters.

Neal J. Palmer
631 Valley Road, Ridley Park, PA 19078
267-345-9090 • NJP@gmail.com

April 8, 2012

Mr. Bill Zoleski
Owner, Victory Brewing Company
420 Acorn Lane
Downingtown, PA 19335

Dear Mr. Zoleski:

First I would like to express my respect and admiration for your very successful brewery. As a fellow home brewer, I find the history of Victory Brewing particularly impressive. You and your colleague Tim Merriman were able to take a common interest and develop it into a business that has earned numerous accolades and awards.

I also share your love of brewing. Over the past several years, my father and I have been active home brewers. We grow our own hops, mill our own grains and develop our own recipes. The smell of malt and hops in a boiling brew kettle in my mind is the smell of victory.

Naturally, when I saw on your website that you were looking for an entry level brand manager, I was immediately interested. The job description states that you seek an individual who is results driven and creative with strong interpersonal and communication skills. I feel that I would be the ideal fit for this position.

Over the past three years, I have attended West Chester University pursuing a marketing degree. I have also worked 30 hours a week at Acme Markets as a Customer Service Representative (CSR). While maintaining a full course load and work schedule, I have earned a 3.2 GPA. As a CSR, I have honed my analytical and communication skills through servicing customers and fellow employees. I have been named Employee of the Month four times in the last seven months.

I also volunteer as the assistant tennis coach for Ridley High School. My experience as a coach has given me the ability to transform 30 different personalities and skill sets into one force.

My attached resume provides greater detail of the qualifications and achievements that would benefit Victory Brewing Co. Please contact me at your earliest convenience to arrange an interview at 267-345-9090. Thank you.

Sincerely,

Neal J. Palmer

CALLOUTS:

[first paragraph]

The author strategically compliments the reader, immediately commanding attention. The reader has probably never read a paragraph like this. Also, the writer begins to develop an immediate connection with the brewery owner—the author is also a brewer.

[second paragraph]

The second paragraph builds upon the chemistry of the first. The employer must love brewing; it's what he does very successfully. The applicant is also a brewer. Perhaps most importantly of all, the author has already created a kind of bond between himself and his reader. The language is poetic, yet not over the top. The author has already virtually guaranteed himself an interview.

[body paragraphs—three through five]

The author takes a risk: he doesn't mention the job opening until the third paragraph. However, in his case, the risk is worth taking because there is no way that the brewery owner stops reading after those killer opening paragraphs. The key to the body paragraphs is that the author creates a match between himself and the job description. He does this quite well and mentions the job description—never a bad idea. He also demonstrates that he has a strong work ethic—instead of vaguely asserting that he possesses this quality—by mentioning that he works nearly a full-time job while attending school full-time and still excelling at his studies. Also, he is clearly an exemplary employee; and he proves it rather than just stating it.

Demonstrating work ethic and work performance are particularly important here. Employers don't want lazy people (often a criticism of millennials particularly) who don't really care about the job. He also takes time from his busy schedule to volunteer. This is powerful. Those who care about others are far more likely to care about their job and employer. Also, coaching is leading and, again, he proves that he has an important qualification—leadership—without using the word. The language used in the final sentence here is sheer poetry.

[final paragraph]

He makes his final paragraph short and sweet. At this point, all he really has to do is ask for an interview and provide contact information. He does that and something else: he mentions that he will benefit the employer. This is important and completely different from typical cover letter. The company wants to know what you can do for them. The more you demonstrate how you can help them grow, the better.

Gabriel Polselli

367 N. Church St. West Chester, PA 19380
(484) 881-9618 GPolselli@gmail.com

July 23, 2009

Mr. Andrew Matthews
Editor, News of Delaware County
251 N. Providence Road
Media, PA 19063

Dear Mr. Matthews:

I would first like to express my profound respect and admiration for the staff and founders of the News of Delaware County. I have read every single issue of the newspaper and have found the writing to be insightful, creative, and overall transcendent of a typical small town newspaper. However, I have noticed that there is one void. Allow me to explain.

Most newspapers that contain town event guides, like Delaware's *Spark*, have a film review section. These sections usually provide a casual, subjective opinion of the current films playing, from the perspective of a local. I am confident that I possess the skills and knowledge to contribute such a column to your event guide.

For the past four years, I have been majoring at West Chester University in Professional Studies and minoring in Film Criticism and Professional Education. I will be graduating in the fall. Classes have ranged from Journalism to The Films of Latin America to The Study of Television Culture to American Themes in Cinema. These academic experiences, along with my genuine passion for film and cinema, have given me the insight and skills necessary to review films for your paper.

Before attending WCU, I grew up right here in the borough. I know the inhabitants of Media, from the Courthouse professionals to the coffee shop regulars to the many store owners. It has always been my dream to write film reviews and I think that, if given the opportunity, I would fit in perfectly with your staff and make a valuable contribution to an exceptional paper.

After you have reviewed my resume, I look forward to an interview to discuss what I can bring to the News of Delaware County. Please contact me at (484) 881-9618 or GPolselli@gmail.com. Thank you.

Sincerely,

Gabe Polselli

COMMENTARY:

First and foremost, this letter demonstrates that there is no known job opening. So why was it written? It's because the author really wants to work for a particular publication. This follows a key principle: write to the companies where you truly want to work and you will write better cover letters and get more interviews. This opening paragraph also strategically schmoozes the employer and takes a risk by offering constructive criticism of the newspaper.

This may be risky, but remember one thing: you have nothing to lose when you write your cover letters. So long as you don't do anything ridiculous, you're OK. What this applicant does is gutsy but, again, strategic: he has to convince the recipient that the publication should have a film review section.

In his second paragraph, he hints at the type of column he would write and references another local publication. As in the first paragraph, the writing is exceptional. This is important: exceptional writing is a powerful differentiator; you will get interviews with killer writing: language that the reader wants to read, but very seldom sees.

The third and fourth paragraphs not only present the author's qualifications but, again, use language that is virtually irresistible. The author demonstrates that he was born to do the job. In a way, he has been preparing for it for years. If you can create this kind of connection between yourself and a prospective employer, you will get interviews.

SHEA MILLER

SHEAMILLER@gmail.com 484.885.6941
6718 Hilltop Drive, Brookhaven, PA 19015

19 March 2012

SAP America
Attn: Kathleen Shaunessy, Human Resources Department
3999 West Chester Pike
Newtown Square, PA 19073

Dear Kathleen Shaunessy:

I would like to first express my admiration and respect for SAP as a global leader in software solutions. I have heard many positive remarks about the company, its corporate structure, and supportive employee culture. SAP perpetually innovates and provides its customers with unsurpassed products and customer service. It is this business structure and philosophy that draw my interest. Also, I had the opportunity to interact with a leader at SAP, Mr. John Milton, while working at a local golf club. He exuded professionalism from our first meeting and fueled my determination to succeed as an individual and in all areas of life. Mr. Milton is the epitome of a business leader who wants to see others succeed.

I am a technology driven individual with an entrepreneurial mindset. Your company's values match my own. I want to contribute to a cutting-edge industry leader that helps to drive the economy and enables businesses to flourish in a rapidly evolving global arena. Having minored in urban planning at West Chester University, I took immediate notice of the new LEED Platinum certified Headquarters. This demonstrates that SAP is a forerunner in sustainability during a time of complicated environmental implications. With my skill set centered on effective business communication, sales, and technology, I am ready to start my career in software sales and consulting at SAP.

I have the desire and ability to absorb new information and communicate effectively to your prospects and clients. The training program will broaden my knowledge of SAP products which, combined with extensive experience in sales/customer interaction, will make me a strong asset. I have worked with many advanced computer programs that also provide me with a solid foundation to interact with and learn how to operate new software suites.

I am currently finishing my last semester at West Chester University. My desire to learn and better myself academically has led to a 3.9 GPA over my last two full-time semesters. I am ready to carry my hard work and discipline into the workplace. My attention to detail and ability to work in a team atmosphere, both exemplified through school and work experiences, will allow me to succeed in a variety of contemporary business settings.

The accompanying resume describes the experience and skill set that I would bring to SAP. I look forward to hearing from you. I can be reached at SHEAMILLER@gmail.com or 484.885.6941. Thank you.

Sincerely,

Shea Miller

CALLOUTS:

[first paragraph]

The opening paragraph acknowledges the employer's stature in the world and shows that the applicant has talked to others about SAP. So he has no doubt conducted some online research, as well as some of his own. The text about McStravick pretty much guarantees an interview (and he did receive one).

[body paragraphs]

The author takes a risk. He doesn't mention the "training program" until the third paragraph. However, he mentions his college minor, but not his major, so he has to prove that he is qualified to be trained in sales by a major international company with very high standards. He does so mainly with very strategic writing—specifically the language of business.

The most impressive business language is highlighted.

24 South Church St. Apt 3H
West Chester, PA 19380

November 3rd, 2013

Ms. Shawn Ziemba, Managing Director
The Mergis Group
500 E Swedesford Road, Suite 100
Wayne, PA 19087

Dear Ms. Ziemba:

In my search for an accounting related position, I reviewed your posting for a junior staff accountant and further explored your website. It appears that while you are involved in a variety of accounting and financial consulting specialties, there is something special about your philosophy. Your genuine relationship with each and every client is important to me because I intend to help people to achieve financial security. Personal portfolio management and ethical consulting advice should focus on the client's best interests, not mine. Because of this shared commitment, I am very interested in the opening within your firm.

I believe that I can be a valued member of your team. Through my studies at West Chester University, I have gained an understanding and appreciation for accurate financial reporting and responsible capital management. Through personal mentoring with my father, a manager of more than 250 personal investment portfolios and himself a self-made millionaire, I have gained knowledge of how to make sound investment decisions. I believe that this know-how will allow me to be an effective and productive member of your consulting team. I will hit the deck running, able to provide valuable consulting advice to a wide range of clients. For this reason, I believe that I would be a good fit for The Mergis Group.

I would also bring a strong work ethic to your firm. Since my sophomore year in high school, I have worked at least 25 hours a week in various jobs. I started as a cashier at my local Acme food store and, within two years, I was promoted to customer service associate at the information desk. This position provided valuable experience in resolving complaints and interacting with customers. Currently, I work at the Aronomink Country Club as a member of the grounds maintenance crew. This job has taught me the value of teamwork. I believe these skills would be valuable in any career field, but especially in consulting.

While working part-time, I have excelled at my studies, earning a 3.16 GPA through my first two years at West Chester University as I pursue a dual major in accounting and finance. I take every opportunity to learn something new very seriously because my career is extremely important to me.

In closing, I can assure you that I would contribute to your firm's growth. I intend to excel in my profession and I look forward to doing so at The Mergis Group. To schedule an interview, please contact me at (215) 287-8122 or af766611@wcupa.edu. Thank you.

Sincerely,

Alex Free

CALLOUTS:

[opening paragraph]

The applicant demonstrates that he conducted research about the company. More importantly, he shows specifically which aspects of the company appeal to him personally. So, right from the beginning of the letter, he is establishing a connection between himself and the employer/job. As a result, the hiring manager will likely keep reading.

[body paragraphs]

In his body paragraphs, the applicant draws from all relevant personal, academic and work experience to demonstrate his qualifications. The relevant mentoring by his grandfather is a detail that will resonate with any reader. Also, he clearly and compellingly demonstrates that, like his prospective employer, he will operate in his clients' best interest, not his own. This will make him more valuable to the firm and, with his philosophy, enable him to succeed and sustain his enthusiasm and dedication to clients over the long haul.

In the author's third paragraph, the applicant does something that isn't easy and that many people wouldn't even attempt. He talks about jobs that others might consider mundane and not true learning experiences. However, the applicant did learn skills and insights from his grocery store and country club experiences that will enable him to work effectively with others, including clients. He does a very good job of "packaging" his experience in a way that relates to the employer's needs.

The applicant also comes across as a hard worker who succeeds in pretty much everything he does. This is the type of individual that most employers want. He also clearly conveys that he takes himself and his career seriously. In doing so, he creates a portrait of a mature young man who will conduct himself with professionalism and empathy—priceless assets, especially in someone so young.

Lauren M. Schultz

236 East Rosedale Avenue, Apt 218 - West Chester, PA 19382
(717) 303-9964 - LS746789@wcupa.edu

November 7, 2013

Molly Watson
160over90
1 South Broad Street
Philadelphia, PA 19102

Dear Ms. Watson:

I would first like to express my deep admiration and respect for both you and your agency. It is no surprise to me that you are consistently rated among the top three ad agencies in Philadelphia. I truly admire your work with clients ranging from Audi to Nike to UCLA. Your company's success speaks for itself with your many awards and growing client roster.

160over90 requires energetic, dedicated, and determined interns, and I strongly believe that I possess those qualities and more. I am a senior English major at West Chester University and will graduate in May 2015. I have held multiple leadership positions in different organizations on campus. During junior year, I was elected Secretary of the Public Relations Student Society of America (PRSSA) and was then elected Vice President for my senior year. I was also elected Vice President of Lambda Pi Eta, the National Communication Honors Society at the end of my junior year. In these positions, I have been able to excel as both a leader and role model. I have effectively performed public speaking, organization, teamwork, and management skills to help these organizations achieve relevance and growth.

In my first internship at Lehigh Valley Talent, I wrote articles for multiple websites, managed various social media accounts, promoted events, and wrote and distributed press releases. In my second and current internship at Brownstein Group, I assist Account Executives in managing numerous clients, including IKEA. I write and distribute press releases, pitch stories, create media lists, collect media clips, manage various social media accounts, and communicate with clients.

While attending West Chester University, I have also worked simultaneous part time jobs at Edgmont Country Club and Mercedes Benz in Devon where I have honed the ability to multitask, manage time, and work seamlessly with both fellow employees and customers in demanding, fast-paced environments. In these demanding positions, I focus on building strong relationships to maximize customer retention and acquisition.

While maintaining a full course load and a full work schedule, I have earned a 3.6 GPA. Through my experiences, I have developed the ability to manage multiple responsibilities simultaneously. My attached resume provides greater detail of the qualifications and achievements that would benefit 160over90. Please contact me at your earliest convenience at (717) 303-9964 to arrange an interview. Thank you.

Sincerely,

Lauren Schultz

Commentary:

This letter violates two key principles of effective cover letter writing: it uses the word "I" far too often and doesn't match qualifications to the employer's stated (is there a job description?) or perceived needs.

However, this is one of those rare cases where the applicant's experiences are so compelling that she will get interviews based on what she has done, in this case, lots of experience directly related to what advertising and public relations professionals do.

But this applicant isn't only well-qualified and ready to kit the ground running. In her fourth paragraph, she shows that she is no stranger to hard work. She has also developed skills that are very important to any employer (see highlighted text).

Richard P. Weiss

113 East Gay Street • Apartment #9 • West Chester, PA 19382
RW739788@wcupa.edu • (908) 448-7290

October 31, 2013

Lisa Barone
Campus Recruiting Manager
KPMG, LLP
1601 Market Street
Philadelphia, PA 19103

Dear Ms. Barone:

I would like to first express my admiration and respect for KPMG as a global leader in professional services for a wide variety of clients. Not only are KPMG employees dedicated to delivering accurate results, but they understand that their responsibility to the client doesn't end with filing tax returns or annual reports. In today's corporate environment, your clients rely heavily on KPMG professionals to go beyond the numbers and provide advisory and consulting services to ensure sustained profitability. I share this desire to go the extra mile and I would be honored to share my energy and dedication with KPMG as a Winter Audit Intern.

My passion for accounting and professional development landed me a position as an accounting intern at the Chester County Community Foundation. This environment has provided me with hands-on experience that has allowed me to develop both my social and technical accounting skills. My responsibilities include posting invoices, entering donations and tracking investment activity, along with responding to numerous emails and phone calls. I also coordinate monthly finance board meetings and the annual audit report. This internship is only one building block in a strong foundation of academic and real world knowledge.

In my four years at West Chester University, I refused to limit myself in any way. This ambitious attitude has allowed me to maintain a 3.9 GPA while participating in a wide array of on and off campus activities. As an Accounting Peer Tutor for the university, I take great pride in helping to transform fellow classmates into independent thinkers. The Friars' Society has taught me to be frugal with my words, and generous with my actions. I have volunteered countless hours at local soup kitchens, Boys and Girls Clubs and charity events throughout the region. This desire to serve others has recently led me to the Good Will Fire Company in West Chester, PA, where I devote any spare time to assisting people in need.

KPMG knows that going the extra step is essential to achieving and maintaining excellence in the Public Accounting field. With my positive attitude, strong work ethic and desire to serve and excel, I will prove that I know what it means to put clients' needs before my own.

After you have reviewed my resume, I look forward to an interview to discuss why I am the right fit for KPMG. Please contact me at (908) 448-7290 or RW739788@wcupa.edu. Thank you.

Sincerely,

Richard P. Weiss

CALLOUTS:

Commentary:

The applicant does a very effective job of demonstrating research of the company and finding something about KPMG that resonates with him that is also important to KPMG. The language feels very genuine so he has already differentiated himself from 99% of other applicants. He says that he will always go the extra step—exceed expectations—and he proves that he will with the rest of his letter.

No only did the applicant choose to apply to KPMG for specific, meaningful reasons, but he chose his current employer in the same way. This demonstrates that he consistently makes decisions for the right reasons. He doesn't just work somewhere; he works there because he really wants to. This is important: he isn't just cranking out cover letters like most people do. He focuses on one company at a time and crafts letters that will resonate with the reader.

Each letter he writes is customized. Each maximizes his chances of getting an interview.

Also, in his third paragraph, he shows "heart and soul" with numerous examples of volunteer work. So he is an individual who genuinely cares about the welfare of others. He is the type of person that every employer wants.

NANCY ENGMAN

233 Cornwallis Dr. • West Chester, PA 19380 • 484.356.9999 • nengman@gmail.com

November 18, 2013

James Mason
Computer Service and Support Manager
FirstTech, Inc.
2640 Hennepin Avenue South
Minneapolis, MN 55408

Dear Mr. Mason:

Based on my robust and directly relevant experience and education, I am confident that I would be the perfect fit for the Apple Remote Support Engineer position posted on JAMF Nation. FirstTech is the company that I want to work for – a company that believes in Apple products as much as I do. I started using the Macintosh platform for Desktop Publishing, and quickly became a lifelong fan. I now own many Apple products, and work in a suburban public school as a Technical Support Specialist. Approximately four years ago, we started using JAMF's Casper Suite, which dramatically simplified my work by enabling me to manage many Mac OS X computers with ease. I would bring valuable experience with both Apple and JAMF products to the position.

I have worked extensively on the Macintosh platform, including system and network configuration, as well as operating system and application support. Currently I am the highest level Mac support person in our department; a good portion of my day is devoted to supporting end users on the phone, via email and remotely by using Apple Remote Desktop and Casper Remote.

I also have extensive hardware support experience; I became an Apple Certified Mac Technician in 2002, and have successfully recertified every year since. This certification enabled the school district to become authorized by Apple as a Self Servicing Provider, which has dramatically reduced the cost of hardware repairs for our Macintosh computers; performing repairs in-house has eliminated the need to purchase the 3-year AppleCare Protection Plan for our computers.

Some years ago, our technology department determined that implementing a more centralized approach to client management would increase efficiency and user satisfaction. I was instrumental in evaluating solutions, and we chose the Casper Suite for managing our Macintosh clients. The Casper Suite implementation has saved hundreds of man-hours in deployment of new equipment each year, and has also facilitated timely deployment of software applications, scripts, and managed settings to our Mac clients. We are currently in the process of expanding this support to iOS devices as well.

Throughout my career in technology, I have demonstrated an ability to learn new technologies and apply them to problem solving. I believe that my background and my responsibilities in my current position, especially my extensive experience supporting end users with myriad hardware and software needs, meet the qualifications you are seeking.

I would enjoy learning more about this position and arranging an interview. I can be reached at 484-356-9999 or nengman@gmail.com Thank you.

Sincerely,

Nancy Engman

Frank Celleri
4798 Vernon Lane • Garnet Valley, PA 19060
frank.celleri@gmail.com • 630-947-5555

November 7, 2013

Linda L. Capone
Tax Manager, BDO Wilmington
270 Presidential Drive
Wilmington, DE 19807

Dear Ms. Capone:

I am writing to express my interest in the Entry Level Staff Accountant position at BDO, posted on West Chester University's Career Development website. After viewing the job description, I conducted research about BDO and discovered that the firm is quite large but still retains a family-oriented culture. Coming from a large close-knit family, and a long line of CPAs, I want to work for a family-oriented firm. Since the time I was a young child, I wanted to be an accountant like my father and uncle. I have observed them devoting long hours to clients during the busy tax season, and I have also seen the rewards. For all these reasons, I would be very interested in exploring the position with BDO Wilmington.

Throughout my nine years of work experience, I have refined my time management skills. I have also developed a strong work ethic by maintaining a 3.5 GPA at West Chester University while working 30-40 hours per week at Franklin Mint Federal Credit Union, and teaching piano lessons. I am a self-motivated individual with excellent attention to detail. I have prepared several personal tax returns and two corporate tax return assignments by hand in class, earning an A on each assignment. Unlike the majority of accounting students, tax is my passion.

I am at my best in a demanding environment. I am adept at juggling and managing multiple activities and a full academic course load. As a musician, I have learned the importance of teamwork by adjusting my style to mesh with the dynamic of the band. I have also fine-tuned my ability to adapt to the circumstances in any situation, facilitate a plan, and meet or exceed expectations as a team. Music has taught me that, with practice and determination, I can overcome any obstacle. The same is true of the world of accounting. I will conquer any challenge, and I am determined to master the accounting skills necessary to help your firm grow.

I hope to utilize my skills at BDO during the hectic upcoming tax season, and for many more to come. With my commitment to meeting or beating deadlines, my dedication and determination to succeed, I feel that I could contribute immediately to your tax department. I look forward to hearing from you to discuss how I can contribute to BDO. I can be reached at 630-947-5555 or frank.celleri@gmail.com. Thank you.

Sincerely,

Frank Celleri

Ryan A. Berry
538 Maple Avenue • Furlong, PA 18925 • 215-989-0977 • ryan.berry99@gmail.com

21 November 2013

Thomas Putin
Philadelphia Teaching Fellows
440 North Broad Street, Suite 222
Philadelphia, PA 19130-4015

Dear Mr. Putin:

I have had a calling to teach for as long as I can remember. During high school, I volunteered at a pre-school. After a few weeks, I was offered a position to work with after school students. I was a high school student, with no experience. During first week, one student was struggling with the concept of money. I pulled change from my pocket, got some candy, and began teaching. Every day, this student would "buy" candy with my money. A week later, this student came in smiling from ear to ear. She hastily ripped open her backpack and showed me a test with a perfect score. From that moment, I knew that I wanted to make a difference in the lives of children. Through the Philadelphia Teaching Fellowship, I believe that I can witness many more of these cherished moments.

While researching information about your prestigious program, I stumbled across two statistics: "Last year, just 58% of Philadelphia students graduated high school on time. Just 1 in 10 of our African American eighth graders is proficient in math." These statistics shocked me. As I graduate with a degree in Mathematics from West Chester University, I want to help those who struggle with math. Children need leaders to encourage them to learn. I am a leader. I wholeheartedly believe in your mission to end a legacy of educational inequity. As a teaching fellow, I will work hard to inspire the youth of Philadelphia. They are our future. Failing to maximize their opportunities to attain knowledge and success is unacceptable.

I have developed my leadership skills through rigorous training as a cadet in Air Force ROTC. As Director of Training, I helped my trainees achieve a 97% graduation rate, while the national average was just 60%. Outside of the 10 hours a week of ROTC, I have worked a combined 30 hours between two jobs. As a pre-school aid, I facilitate classroom learning and motivate young children. As the general manager of Peace Valley Boat Rental, I train all staff members. I am also an efficient time manager. Even with 10 hours of ROTC and 30 hours of work weekly, I have achieved a 3.6 GPA.

If I became a Fellowship Member, I would pass on my leadership, and learn from those around me. I look forward to discussing my calling to teach with you in an interview. I can be reached at 215-989-0977 or ryan. berry99@gmail.com. Thank you.

Very Respectfully,

Ryan A. Berry

CHAPTER 6

Effective Resume Examples

Resume Tips

By the way, you can have a relatively weak resume and an exceptional cover letter and you'll get interviews. One reason: exceptional writing is rare and highly valued by companies. Conversely, most large companies cite writing as their employees' biggest weakness.

- Avoid templates. They can make your text too small, limit your flexibility in getting your resume on one page and make your text difficult to edit.

- Consider including a profile or summary of qualifications near the top (see samples).

- Only use an objective if it's written to show how you'll benefit the company; you can customize the objective with the company name.

- One of the first things the hiring manager looks for is your education. So place education section near top of resume.

- Never use first person point of view (I, me, my).

- Include "heart and soul" experience, e.g., volunteering, fundraising for a worthy cause and serving in the military. Your job application materials will be read by a human being; they'll react to emotional content in a human way. Also, people who care about others are most likely to care about their job and employer.

- Only include college courses if you need to fill in space and make your resume look more substantial.

- Only include hobbies if they are directly relevant to the position. If they are, definitely include them as they will be a differentiator.

- "Package" what you've done in the most businesslike and compelling way (in both cover letter and resume). For example, let's say you work at a restaurant. The restaurant industry has the highest failure rate and what you do is critical to customer retention and acquisition through positive word of mouth—based on your ability to deliver exceptional customer service and satisfaction. You're working for a business, so don't be afraid to characterize your experience in a way that every businessperson can relate to and appreciate.

LAUREN SCHULTZ
717.303.9964
LS746789@WCUPA.EDU

CURRENT ADDRESS
2300 EAST ROSEDALE AVE, APT. 299
WEST CHESTER, PA 19382

PERMANENT ADDRESS
1942 THOMAS STREET
HARRISBURG, PA 17112

EDUCATION
West Chester University of Pennsylvania, West Chester, PA
Bachelor of Arts in Communication Studies, Anticipated May 2014
- GPA: 3.646, Dean's Lists

PROFESSIONAL EXPERIENCE
Boyd Tamney Cross, Wayne, PA
Public Relations Internship, May 2013-Present
- Assisting VP of Public Relations
- Writing and releasing pitches and press releases for multiple clients
- Managing various Facebook accounts
- Creating media lists using Cision
- Writing articles for clients intended for numerous types of media outlets

Brandywine Valley Talent, Chadds Ford, PA
Communications Internship, May 2012-October 2012
- Wrote press releases and articles for multiple websites
- Managed multiple Facebook, Twitter and Pinterest accounts
- Created and ran Facebook ads to attract clients
- Designed showcase invitations using Microsoft Office programs

ADDITIONAL EXPERIENCE
Concord Country Club, West Chester, PA
Server, May 2012-Present
- Breakfast, lunch, and dinner server in dining room and banquets for over 200 people
- Co-manager of pool snack bar
- Provide customer service to brides and bridal parties as the bridal suite attendant

Porsche of the Mainline, West Chester, PA
Receptionist, January-October 2013
- Answered and directing phone calls
- Utilized Excel and w.e.b. suite to track customer transactions
- Provided friendly customer service to every client

Kohl's, Harrisburg, PA
Cashier/Customer Service Representative, September 2009-April 2012
- Top solicitor for store credit cards and emails

ACTIVITIES AND LEADERSHIP
PRSSA (Public Relations Student Society of America), WCU
Vice President, 2012-Present
- Organize and plan meetings, events, and trips to network with Public Relations professionals
- Manage member committees
- Plan and run chapter meetings
- Working as a team with the executive board *SAIL*
- SAIL *(Students Actively Involved in Leadership)*, WCU
- Attend workshops and programs to develop leadership skills

Lambda Pi Eta, WCU
Vice President, 2013-Present
- Maintain GPA requirement
- Plan, organize, and participate in events on and off campus
- Develop new programs for students in the Communication Studies program

Women Leading Up, WCU
- Attend workshops and programs to learn tips and skills for becoming a leading female professional

Richard P. Weiss

113 East Gay Street • Apartment #9•West Chester, PA 19382
(908) 448-7290 • RW739788@wcupa.edu • www.Linkedin.com/in/richardweiss

Education:

West Chester University of Pennsylvania, West Chester, PA
Exp. Graduation: May 2015

- Bachelor of Science, Accounting (150 Credits)
- AACSB Accredited Business School
- Minor in Criminal Justice
- **Dean's List all semesters; GPA: 3.9**

Professional Experience:

Learning Assistance and Resource Center, West Chester University
Accounting Peer Tutor: April 2013-Present

- Assist fellow undergraduate students during weekly, one hour tutoring sessions
- Maintain accurate schedules, attendance records and progress reports
- Participate in monthly training seminars and biweekly departmental meetings with supervisors

Chester County Community Foundation, West Chester, PA
Accounting Intern: November 2012-Present

- Responsible for posting expense invoices to the accounts payable software system
- Thoroughly research and examine Non-Profit Organizations being awarded monetary grants
- Employ proficient use of Microsoft Excel, Financial Edge and Raiser's Edge software programs

West Chester University of Pennsylvania, West Chester, PA
Resident Assistant: September 2011-May 2013

- Helped residents connect with the resources and organizations that interest them
- Designed and implemented various social and educational programs for the students
- Enforced Pennsylvania State Law and University Policies within the residence hall

Open and Close Pool Service, Manahawkin, NJ
Pool Service Supervisor: May 2010-May 2013

- Managed and reviewed weekly chemical and cleaning schedules for all 100 clients
- Accurately appraised costs of maintenance, repair and installation work
- Demanded proficient interpersonal skills with clients and co-workers

Community/University Involvement:

Good Will Fire Company, West Chester, PA
September 2013-Present

- Volunteer Firefighter
- **Elko and Associates, Ltd., 2013 Summer Leadership Program**
  May 2013
- Four day program exploring Audit, Tax and Advisory practices

Friars' Honorary Service Society of West Chester University
April 2012-Present

- Social Chair (2012-2013)
- Board of the Brotherhood Member (2013-2014)

Leadership Experience:

- Participant in the Enterprise Global Leadership Series: Spring 2013
- Participant in the State Farm Student Leadership Experience: Spring 2013
- Peer Mentor for the College of Business and Public Affairs Peer Mentorship Program: Spring 2013
- Student Member of the American Institute of Certified Public Accountants

NANCY ENGMAN

233 Cornwallis Dr. • West Chester, PA 19380 • 484.356.9999 • nengman@gmail.com

Experience

West Chester Area School District – West Chester, PA   9/97–Present

Technical Support Specialist (9/00–Present)
- Support technology users in 16 district schools and central administration building
- Maintain and support Macintosh and Windows laptop and desktop systems
- Perform all warranty and non-warranty repairs for 2500+ Macintosh computers
- Configure and deploy standard installation configurations for new computer and mobile device systems
- Utilized client management tools to automate remote support, installations, and inventory reporting
- Train technology personnel in troubleshooting techniques

Help Desk Technician (12/99–9/00)
- Provided telephone and on-site support and troubleshooting for applications and hardware
- Delivered training, support and assistance to teachers using technology in the classroom
- Installed and configured software for new and existing computers
- Developed training documentation

Technology Associate (9/97–12/99)
- Supported technology including computers, printers and other peripherals at middle school with 850+ users
- Assisted students and teachers in computer lab, and administered lab network
- Set up new computers and equipment; installed and configured software; performed hardware upgrades
- Analyzed technology needs and advised on purchasing for instruction and administration

Sir Speedy Printing–Exton, PA   11/94–9/97

Graphic Artist/Systems Manager
- Designed a variety of artwork for customers, including logos, business stationery, flyers, brochures, postcards, newsletters and annual reports.
- Maintained network of seven computers; troubleshot hardware and software issues
- Evaluated and advised on purchase of new software and hardware

Busy Bytes–West Chester, PA   4/92–11/94

Typographer
- Delivered layout of documents and designed artwork for clients based upon supplied specifications
- Purchased and maintained computer and software for home based business
- Worked independently to deliver completed projects on time

Unisys Corporation, Defense Systems–Paoli, PA   10/84–4/90

Data Processing Consultant (9/89–4/90)
- Coordinated transition of manufacturing test system to two new plants
- Acted as liaison between plants and trained new personnel
- Achieved goal of smooth transition to new facility with minimal downtime during transition, minimal startup time at new plants and adherence to contractual deadlines

Engineering Programmer (9/85–11/88)
- Designed, developed and implemented software and instrumentation for product testing
- Devised test system for use on multiple products which reduced times for development, testing and training
- Supported end users in plant

Programmer (10/84–9/85)
- Increased productivity by automating paperwork, report and presentation functions of Engineering department
- Created data base for tracking incoming parts, which assisted management in meeting deadlines

Education

West Chester University of Pennsylvania, West Chester, PA   9/80–12/87, 9/12–Present
Bachelor of Science, Computer Science, Degree expected May 2014

Pennsylvania State University, State College, PA–World Campus Online   01/01–04/01
6 credits earned towards Instructional Technology Certificate

Technical Skills

Certifications: Apple Certified Macintosh Technician (ACMT)
Hardware: Macintosh and Windows desktops and laptops (Dell, Lenovo, HP), Printers, Document Cameras
Operating Systems: Mac OS X, Microsoft Windows 2000 and newer, Unix
Software: Casper Client Management, Microsoft Office, Active Directory, Adobe CS, Java

Frank Celleri
4798 Vernon Lane • Garnet Valley, PA 19060
frank.celleri@gmail.com • 630-947-5555

EDUCATION:
Bachelor of Science, Accounting. Degree anticipated Spring 2014 with 150 credit hours from West Chester University of Pennsylvania, West Chester, PA
- **19383 AACSB Certified**
- **Current GPA - 3.1**
- **Accounting GPA - 3.56**

EXPERIENCE:
Flagship Credit Acceptance, Aug. 2012 to Present
Position: Funding Analyst
- Input financial data for record keeping and auto loan structure utilizing Excel and APM
- Consolidate new auto loans received by FedEx to begin the funding process
- Verify customer insurance, employment, and income to ensure accurate documentation
- Establish contact with new customers via phone to verify contract terms

Frank Coppola's Guitar Teaching, Sept. 2007 to Present
Position: Self-employed guitar teacher of all ages
- Manage all scheduling of clients
- Attract new clients through self promotion and marketing tools
- Provide group and private lessons to students ages 5+
- Utilize Microsoft Excel to maintain financial activity of the business

P.F. Chang's, Glen Mills, PA, September 2011 to May 2012
Position: Back Waiter
- Responsible for maintaining cleanliness of the kitchen/operations area
- Delivered customer orders throughout the restaurant
- Satisfied any customer requests to provide an exceptional dining experience

Meijer, Oswego, IL, April 2007 to Sept. 2010
Position: Planograms/Receiving Associate
- Reset planograms on a daily basis throughout the entire store
- Organized the backroom to maintain efficiency of daily business operations
- Unloaded grocery trucks, and checked in food and alcohol vendors into the receiving area to account for newly received inventory
- Provided customers with exceptional customer service to ensure a satisfying shopping experience

Achievements:
- Completed Microsoft Excel Proficiency Exam at West Chester University
- Published "The Importance of the Cash Flow Statement" http://www.articlesbase.com/accounting-articles/the-importance-of-the-statement-of-cash-flow-6699999.html

Activities:
- Guitar: Twelve years of playing, reading and writing music on the guitar. Also knowledgeable in guitar repair, as well as providing services for music recording/production.
- West Chester University of Pennsylvania Accounting Society

Ryan A. Berry

538 Maple Avenue • Furlong, PA 18925 • 215-989-0977 • ryan.berry99@gmail.com

---

Education

West Chester University of Pennsylvania
Bachelor of Science in Mathematics • Graduation May, 2014 • GPA 3.6

Professional Leadership Experience

General Manager
Bucks County Department of Parks and Recreation, Doylestown, PA   May 2007-Present

- Foster customer relations and retention
- Enforce county regulations including watercraft safety, medical training
- Ingrain enthusiasm and integrity in the training of 21 staff members

Pre-School Assistant Teacher
Community Educational Centers, Doylestown, PA   September 2008-Present

- Develop and implement lessons for children ages 2-7

Air Force Reserve Officer Training Corps
USAF ROTC Detachment 750   August 2009-Present

- Professional training to groom future US Air Force Officers
- Developed leadership and followership skills; core values of Integrity, Service, Excellence
- Successfully completed AFROTC Field Training in August 2011

Watercraft Safety Program Organizer
Bucks County Department of Parks and Recreation, Doylestown, PA   June 2010-Present

- Implemented classes to train children ages 10-17

Director of Training
Air Force Reserve Officer Training Corps, Philadelphia, PA   August 2011-December 2011

- Motivated and led young adults to become leaders
- 97% AF Field Training graduation rate; national average was 60%
- Developed syllabi and lesson plans

Volunteer Work

Community Educational Centers – Summer Camp Counselor

- Facilitated activities to enhance the learning of kindergarten age children

Arnold Air Society – Commander

- Prisoner of War/Missing in Action community runs, Merion Train Station Clean-Up, Merion Botanical Park Clean-Up, Operation Philabundance, Broad Street Run, Philadelphia Marathon

---

Awards and Recognition

- Airlift and Tanker Association Essay Scholarship Recipient, 2013
- Detachment 750 Warrior Spirit Award, 2011
- AFROTC Scholarship Recipient, 2009

Lindsey Lacey

110 West Manor Way—Robbinsville, NJ 08691

Cell (609) 647-8888—LL674399@wcupa.edu

OBJECTIVE

To obtain a marketing internship providing the opportunity to demonstrate strong work ethic, reliability, organizational and interpersonal skills, as well as gain experience in the marketing field

EDUCATION

West Chester University of Pennsylvania, West Chester, PA, *BS Marketing*, May 2012

Dean's List every semester; GPA 3.98; Outstanding Marketing Junior Award 2010-2011

LEADERSHIP EXPERIENCE

American Marketing Association, Fall 2008 to present, *Co-President (two years)*

Professional student networking and learning organization in marketing field

- Effectively use communication and leadership skills to motivate members to contribute
- Scheduled professionals to speak at meetings and other activities to increase membership

West Chester University, Fall 2010 to present, *College of Business Dean's Advisory Board*

- Selected to represent marketing interests of approximately 200 majors to dean's office

State Farm® Executive Leadership Series, Fall 2009 to Spring 2010

Active Participant in Ongoing Leadership Development Program

Student Leadership Retreat, 10/20/09, *Participant in Freshman Retreat*

- Actively participated in leadership programs; developed social network with other freshmen

PROFESSIONAL EXPERIENCE

Association Headquarters, Inc., [location], Internship - August 9, 2011 to present

- Build new sponsorship sales and marketing prospect database to target new revenue opportunities
- Collaborate on new business development proposals, conference marketing, membership growth, and new sponsorship sales ideas
- Identify and track 3 ways of measuring marketing success of MarCom campaigns
- Learned how to utilize social media sites
- Evaluated marketing proposals
- Learned how to segment markets and find new markets to tap

Sun Splash Jewelry, Long Beach Island, NJ, 06/2007 to present, *Shift Manager, Sales Representative*

- Managed 3 individuals in a small company
- Effectively addressed customer and employee concerns
- Recognized as one of top employees

Creative Marketing Alliance, Princeton Junction, NJ, 12/09 to 01/10, *Marketing Intern*

- Contributed to direct mail, social media, and in-house marketing projects
- Gained valuable experience in the field of marketing

COMMUNITY SERVICE

West Chester University Circle K (Extension of Kiwanis), Fall 2008 to present, *Club Member*

- Breast Cancer Walk, AIDS Walk, Adopt-a-Block, Salvation Army Food Drive
- **Students Actively Involved in Leadership (SAIL)**–non-credit leadership development program 1/20/09 to present

CHAPTER 7

Final Words

As you can see, various job applicants have applied principles illustrated and discussed in the classroom to write killer job application materials of such exceptional and compelling quality that they clearly stand out from 99% of the "competition."

Remember that hiring managers and recruiters are accustomed to seeing job application materials that are easy to reject because they don't stand out.

However, what is required of you isn't easy. It takes trust to believe that the best way to get interviews is to focus on one opportunity at a time and only apply for jobs you really want. This seems risky because it would seem that you're minimizing your chances of getting interviews (there are all these jobs on the web; shouldn't I apply for as many as I can?). Go ahead. But you won't get many interviews that way because it's easy to reject hastily written job application materials—which is how you'll write them if you apply to one job after another very quickly without doing at least some of the things recommended and showcased in this manual.

Maximizing your chances of getting interviews for the jobs you really want also takes time, focus and excellent writing. It could take hours for each opportunity. But the time invested is worth it if it pays off.

Above all, spend time reading and rereading the sample letters and resumes in this manual. They are based on the work and feedback provided by former students who were inspired by the work of previous students and tried to make their cover letters in particular even better than what others had done.

Consider what these applicants say in their letters. Can you mimic their strategies but, of course, customize your letter so that it works well and is based on your qualifications and experience…as well as the position you're applying for?

You will get interviews—but only if you do the things recommended in this manual.

Are you up to the challenge? You'll have to be if you really want the job of your dreams.

CHAPTER 8

Additional Tips to Get Interviews

- **Hand-deliver letter/resume**
  You will almost certainly be required to apply for most positions, even you have been referred or recommended. But hand delivering your job application materials, whenever possible, is a differentiator. It shows that you are interested because you got off your butt and drove to the place. Also, your materials will be separate from everyone else's—from that huge pile that the hiring manager has to wade through.

- **Follow up**
  After most people apply for a job, they do nothing. Wait a week and then email or call. This shows interest. Better yet, email them something of interest to their company, industry, whatever. Show that you're thinking about them because you want to work there.

- **Send customized thank you letter(s)**
  Take notes during the interview(s). Make sure you get everyone's name and title. Place notes under each person's name so you can customize your thank you letter based on things they say in the interview. Think about what they have said and play it back to them, possibly with your thoughts about the issue discussed—maybe even a possible solution to a problem.

- **Send thank you letter after rejection**
  This sounds counter-intuitive, but another position may open up in the same company or the recipient of your thank you note may hear of a job elsewhere. Very few people thank someone after being rejected; you will stand out and something good may occur.

Dear Professor Scholl:

I ran into my cousin's best friend, Tim Treston, who is in his late 20s, out in town one night and I went up to him to talk. We started getting into what we were doing and turned out he was a senior financial analyst at Lockheed Martin. He asked me what year I was and I told him I am finishing up next May and looking for an internship. He said to send him my resume, so I did and that is where it began.

Once, I sent him my resume, he called the head recruiter at LMC's Cherry Hill branch, Fred Shawver. He said there was a non-tech internship for Finance and Accounting majors that just opened up and for me to apply online. I applied online and asked you for the next step on what would differentiate me from the other applicants. You said the next step would be to hand deliver my cover letter and resume directly to Fred Shawver. I called Tim Treston to see what his thoughts were about this and he told me that it would be hard to meet with him because of the security at LMC. After, I went back to you and you said to still go down there and drop it off to the front desk if he was not available.

The next day I put on my suit and tie and went down to Cherry Hill with my cover letter and resume enclosed in an envelope addressed to Fred Shawver. Once I got down there, the doors were locked and there were two security guards at the desk. They decided to let me in because I guess I don't look like too bad of a guy and asked them if Fred Shawver was available. The security guard gave him a call and turns out he was not busy. He came down the elevator and I introduced myself. We talked for a few minutes and at the end he told me his colleague or he would give me a call later in the week for a phone interview.

He stuck to his word and his colleague, James Reynolds, gave me a call for a phone interview. The interview lasted for ten minutes and, at the end of the interview, James told me that he would email me with more forms that I had to fill out before I could get started. He emailed me with forms and one of the forms was my offer letter. Two days later I received my official offer letter in the mail and I accepted immediately.

I believe the only reason I got this internship is because I listened to you and took the time to go meet with Fred Shawver with my resume and cover letter. I differentiated myself from the other 200 applicants and it paid off.

I appreciate everything that you have taught me over this semester. I am very fortunate to have you as a teacher and believe without the things you have stressed so much in class that I would be back to being a mover again for the summer. Thank you for a great semester and I hope you have an awesome summer.

Sincerely,

Brian Lawlor
Bachelor of Science, Finance

About
RICHARD J. SCHOLL

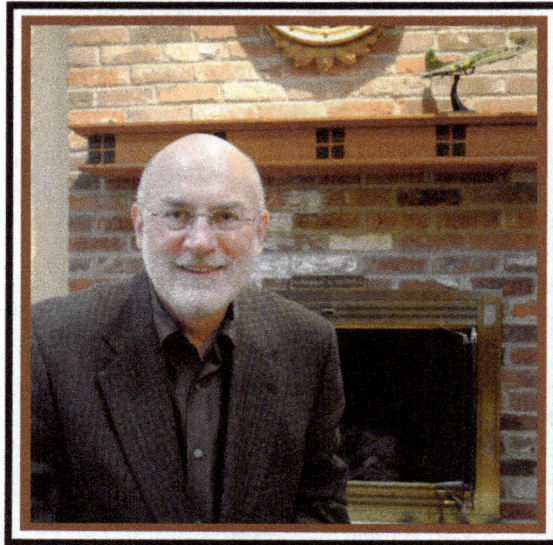

Adjunct Professor of English, West Chester University of Pennsylvania
Adjunct Professor of Marketing, Villanova University
President & Creative Director, The Scholl Group

To learn more about Richard J. Scholl please visit:
http://www.theSchollGroup.com

Richard J. Scholl has more than a quarter century of experience in teaching at the university level as well as more than 35 years of business communications and marketing experience. He has taught business writing courses at both Drexel University and West Chester of Pennsylvania for more than 15 years. He also teaches marketing courses at Villanova University.

Richard is president and creative director of The Scholl Group, a full service marketing and advertising firm whose clients have included AAA, Aetna/US Healthcare, Discovery Communications, Disney, Educational Testing Service, Hasbro, International Reading Association, Lenox, Mattel, NOVO 1, QVC, 7-Eleven, The Franklin Institute and Vanguard.

Author of eight books on a wide variety of topics, Richard is also a corporate writing coach (see schollwritingcoach.com). His greatest passion is to help others get the jobs of their dreams and succeed by strategically employing writing and communications skills to enhance their organizations, clients and customers and themselves.